*Each of the Fruits of the Spirit
is but a Phase of Love.*

Joy is love exulting.

Peace is love reposing.

Patience is love enduring.

Goodness is the good manners of love.

Kindness is love in action.

Faithfulness is love confiding.

Gentleness is love yielding.

Self-Control is true self-love.

A.W. Tozer

Words Worth Remembering

A collection of scripture, songs, and inspirational quotations

By Susan McGeown

Faith Inspired Books

Faith Inspired Books

Published by Faith Inspired Books

3 Kathleen Place, Bridgewater, New Jersey 08807

susanmcgeown@faithinspiredbooks.com

www.FaithInspiredBooks.com

Copyright November 16, 2017

All Rights Reserved

ISBN: 978-1-946268-02-0

ISBN-10: 1-946268-02-X

Bibliographic credit appears at the end of this work.

Christmas, 2017

Dearest Friends,

I find it a bit funny that for all the years I've been writing, my greatest sales revenues have been these end-of-the-year gift books I've been giving out to my friends for free as Christmas gifts. You should know, I spend the whole year 'waiting' for 'the Spirit' to give me the new theme. It's no use trying to force it or do it early; it arrives in my mind when it arrives and there's nothing a girl can do about it. Of the initial two ideas I toyed with, I *tried* mightily to cram them into the monthly/year book style that I've done in the past, but no go. ('A Year of Blessings' and 'A Year With The Spirit' sits dusty and unfinished in my computer. Maybe next year?) No, when the idea finally came for this year's book it was a departure from my previous two endeavors. This year, I'm giving you a collection of Scripture verses, song lyrics, and inspirational quotes that are near and dear to my heart.

I've been collecting words for almost fifty years; long before I was a teacher or an author or a public speaker. It all started in my early teens with scripture and song lyrics that especially touched me and over the years it has morphed into a huge library of handwritten journals that I usually only make use of in my stories, presentations, and Bible studies.

Many of these words are so precious to me that I've committed them to memory (which in some cases took years!). Almost every Scripture verse noted in this book I know by heart (but usually can't remember the biblical reference … grrr). I'm not bragging; I just want you to know how much these words have become a part of me.

I didn't anticipate how stressful this experience has turned out to be! Which ones do I include and which ones do I keep out? What if I forget a very essential one once I've pushed the publish button? Are the words I've chosen the right ones to speak to those who will pick up this book? What if these words aren't as profound for others as they are for me? What if…? (God told me to stop stalling at this point and get writing…!)

I've made every effort to footnote the origination of these quotes and any errors are completely of my own making. Scripture verses, unless otherwise noted, will be from my favorite Bible translation – the New Living Translation. Please refer to my Bibliography and Footnotes section for specifics.

It is my hope that this year's book will be inspiring to you in a number of ways. I hope that as a result of reading these chosen words you will be eager to:

- Memorize a precious Scripture verse or two or three …,

- Purchase a devotional (*and complete it*) by one of the numerous men and women who have been quoted,

- Read your Bible more in the hopes of building a collection of your own favorite Scripture verses,

- Download and listen to some of the songs (some are hymns and some are contemporary Christian rock) that I've provided the lyrics for, and/or

- Become curious about spiritual things and write any thoughts that come to mind in the MY NOTES section at the end of this book).

Finally, thank you for your love, support, prayers, and encouragement which is a constant blessing to me and mine. I couldn't be the Woman After God's Own Heart (I Samuel 13:14) that I am without you all. May the Holy Spirit bless you as you read this book!

Love,

Sue

> ### Philippians 1:20-21
>
> I eagerly expect and hope that I will in no way be ashamed, but will have sufficient courage so that now as always Christ will be exalted in my body, whether by life or by death. For to me, to live is Christ and to die is gain.

Table of Contents

whatever is:

true

noble

right

pure

lovely

admirable

excellent

praiseworthy

[think on these things]

(Philippians 4:8)

SONGS

COUNT YOUR MANY BLESSINGS NAME THEM ONE BY ONE COUNT YOUR MANY BLESSINGS SEE WHAT GOD HAS DONE

Susan McGeown

The Servant Song[1]

*I've only heard this sung once or twice in church
but its words are so moving!!
I just love the strong theme that we are all in this together.*

Brother, sister let me serve you.
Let me be as Christ to you.
Pray that I might have the grace
To let you be my servant, too.
We are pilgrims on a journey.
We are brothers on the road.
We are here to help each other
Walk the mile and bear the load.
I will hold the Christ-light for you
In the night time of your fear.
I will hold my hand out to you;
Speak the peace you long to hear.
I will weep when you are weeping.
When you laugh, I'll laugh with you.
I will share your joy and sorrow
Till we've seen this journey through.
When we sing to God in heaven,
We shall find such harmony
Born of all we've known together
Of Christ's love and agony.
Brother, sister let me serve you.
Let me be as Christ to you.
Pray that I might have the grace
To let you be my servant, too.

2

One Trick Pony[2]

"If I hear just one more time that I should be more open minded, I think I might scream.
This world says this is all there is yet I believe the One who says there's life after this.
Now tell me, how much more open can my mind be?!" A.M.E.N.!

I'm a one trick pony, if you will
I got a one track mind with a heart that's real
And don't forget I've got tunnel vision
For something much bigger than superstition
Call me hard headed for the One that changed me
Say what you will, it will not phase me
No need for anything up my sleeve
There's just one thing that I'll ever need

You are my one and only
You are my one and only
Oh, I'm a one trick pony

If I hear just one more time
That I should try and be more open-minded
I think I just might scream
The word says this is all there is
Yet I believe the One who says there's life after this
Now tell me how much more open can my mind be?

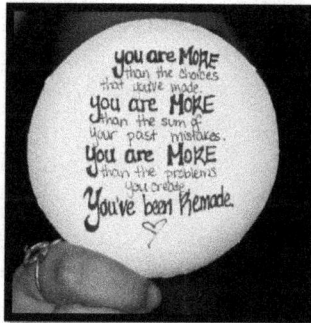

Susan McGeown

Hymn[3]

It's hard to believe that this is a Christian rock song, but it is. (Which is one of the reasons I love the band Jars of Clay so much.) "Oh gaze of love so melt my pride, that I may in Your house but kneel..." should be everyone's personal prayer, don't you think?

Oh refuge of my hardened heart
Oh fast pursuing lover come
As angels dance around Your throne
My life by captured fare You own
Not silhouette of trodden faith
Nor death shall not my step be guide
I'll pirouette upon my grave
For in Your path I'll run and hide
Oh gaze of love so melt my pride
That I may in Your house but kneel
And in my brokenness to cry
Spring worship unto Thee
When beauty breaks the spell of pain
The bludgeoned heart shall burst in vain
But not when love be pointed king
And truth shall Thee forever reign
Oh gaze of love so melt my pride
That I may in Your house but kneel
And in my brokenness to cry
Spring worship unto Thee
Sweet Jesus carry me away
Form cold of night and dust of day
In ragged hour or salt worn eye
Be my desire, my well spring lie
Oh gaze of love so melt my pride
That I may in Your house but kneel
And in my brokenness to cry
Spring worship unto Thee
Oh gaze of love so melt my pride
That I may in Your house but kneel
And in my brokenness to cry
Spring worship unto Thee.

4

<u>Great Is Thy Faithfulness</u>[4]

This was sung at my wedding.
It's one of our favorite hymns.
"Morning by morning new mercies I see..."
Thank you, God.

Great is Thy faithfulness, O God my Father
There is no shadow of turning with Thee
Thou changest not, Thy compassions, they fail not
As Thou hast been, Thou forever will be

Great is Thy faithfulness
Great is Thy faithfulness
Morning by morning new mercies I see
All I have needed Thy hand hath provided
Great is Thy faithfulness, Lord, unto me

Summer and winter and springtime and harvest
Sun, moon and stars in their courses above
Join with all nature in manifold witness
To Thy great faithfulness, mercy and love

Great is Thy faithfulness
Great is Thy faithfulness
Morning by morning new mercies I see
All I have needed Thy hand hath provided
Great is Thy faithfulness, Lord, unto me

Pardon for sin and a peace that endureth
Thine own dear presence to cheer and to guide
Strength for today and bright hope for tomorrow
Blessings all mine, with ten thousand beside.

Awakening[5]

This is my Life's Theme Song.

Dress down your pretty faith, give me something real
Leave out the Thee and Thou and speak to me now
Speak to my pain and confusion
Speak through my fears and my pride
Speak to the part of me that knows I'm something deep down inside

I know that I'm not perfect, but compare me to most
In a world of hurt in a world of anger I think I'm holding my own
And I know that you've said there is more to life
No I am not satisfied
But there are mornings I wake up and I'm just thankful to be alive

I've known for quite a while that I am not whole
I've remembered the body and the mind, but dissected the soul
Now something inside is awakening
Like a dream I once had and forgot
And it's something I'm scared of and something I don't want to stop

I woke up this morning and realized, Jesus is not a portrait
Or stained glass windows, Or hymns
Or all the tradition that surrounds us
I thought it would be hard to believe in, but it's not hard at all
To believe I've sinned, And fallen short
Of the glory of God

He's not asking me to change in my joy for martyrdom
He's asking to take my place
To stand in the gap that I have formed
With His real amazing grace

And it's not just a sign or a sacrament
It's not just a metaphor for love
The blood is real and it's not just a symbol of our faith.

6

<u>Blessings</u>[6]

This isn't a song you can truly appreciate until you're ... older.
After you realize that life, in general, is hard work
with lots of unexpected twists and turns and tragedies.
And only if you've stepped out on faith a time or two and believe that, no matter what,
the Spirit is always with you to comfort, protect, advise, and guide.
Know this: No truer words have ever been sung.

We pray for blessings, we pray for peace
Comfort for family, protection while we sleep
We pray for healing, for prosperity
We pray for Your mighty hand to ease our suffering
All the while, You hear each spoken need
Yet love is way too much to give us lesser things.
'Cause what if Your blessings come through raindrops?
What if Your healing comes through tears?
What if a thousand sleepless nights are what it takes to know You're
near?
What if trials of this life are Your mercies in disguise?
We pray for wisdom, Your voice to hear.
We cry in anger when we cannot feel You near.
We doubt Your goodness, we doubt Your love.
As if every promise from Your Word is not enough.
All the while, You hear each desperate plea,
And long that we'd have faith to believe.
When friends betray us, when darkness seems to win,
We know that pain reminds this heart
That this is not our home.
What if my greatest disappointments,
Or the aching of this life,
Is the revealing of a greater thirst
This world can't satisfy?
What if trials of this life;
The rain, the storms, the hardest nights
Are Your mercies in disguise?

It Is Well With My Soul[7]

I wear a ring all the time that is engraved with the words,
"It is well."
That's how important this song is to me.
Because, no matter what, it is well with my soul.

When peace, like a river, attendeth my way,
When sorrows like sea billows roll;
Whatever my lot, Thou hast taught me to say,

It is well, it is well with my soul.
It is well, With my soul
It is well, it is well with my soul

Though Satan should buffet, though trials should come,
Let this blest assurance control,
That Christ has regarded my helpless estate,
And hath shed His own blood for my soul

My sin, oh, the bliss of this glorious thought!
My sin, not in part but the whole,
is nailed to the cross, and I bear it no more,
praise the Lord, praise the Lord, O my soul!

And, Lord, haste the day when my faith shall be sight,
the clouds be rolled back as a scroll;
the trump shall resound, and the Lord shall descend,
even so, it is well with my soul.

> Because the truth is,
> it doesn't really matter who
> I used to be. It's all about
> who I've become.

Doubly Good To You[8]

I believe this is the first contemporary Christian rock song I ever listened to.
It brought tears to my eyes with its truth and beauty.
He has been doubly good to me. How about you?

If you see the moon, Rising gently on your fields
If the wind blows softly on your face
If the sunset lingers, While the cathedral bells peal
And the moon has risen to her place

You can thank the Father, For the things he has done
Thank Him for the things He's yet to do
And if you find a love that's tender
If you find someone who's true, Thank the Lord
He's been doubly good to you

If you look in the mirror, At the end of a hard day
And you know in your heart you have not lied
If you gave love freely, If you earned an honest wage
And if you've got Jesus by your side

You can thank the father, For the things He has done
And thank him for the things He's yet to do
And if you find a love that's tender
If you find someone who's true, Thank the Lord
He's been doubly good to you

You can thank the father, For the things He has done
And thank him for the things He's yet to do
And if you find a love that's tender
If you find someone who's true, Thank the Lord
He's been doubly good to you

Thank the Lord
He's been doubly good to you

Susan McGeown

Amazing Grace[9]

My favorite verse is the last one:
"When we've been there ten thousand years…"
I'll be singing it at my funeral with a big grin on my face.

Amazing grace! how sweet the sound,
That saved a wretch; like me!
I once was lost, but now am found,
Was blind, but now I see.

'Twas grace that taught my heart to fear,
And grace my fears relieved;
How precious did that grace appear
The hour I first believed

The Lord hath promised good to me,
His word my hope secures;
He will my shield and portion be
As long as life endures.

When we've been there ten thousand years,
Bright shining as the sun,
We've no less days to sing God's praise
Than when we first begun

> You are more than the choices
> that you've made.
> You are more than the sum of
> your past mistakes.
> You are more than the problems
> you create.
>
> "You Are More" by Tenth Avenue North

Sacred Delight[10]

I was driving in my car when I first heard this one. That line,
"Is it true I'm Your heartbeat and
You chose to die than to live without me?" just blew me away.
I pulled over on the side of the road
and sat for the longest time overwhelmed with the truth of it.

Did you smile when you made the moon
And gave the sky its color?
Did creation dance in rhythm to
Your song of life, I wonder?
Did the angels know you knew my name
Before I existed?
Did you tell them out of all you made
Why you gave me your image?

Is it true I'm your heartbeat?
And you love me more than anything?

What sacred delight
What infinite wonder
That I'm precious in Your sight
You love me like no other, no other
Oh, sacred delight

Did you think of me the day you died
That I would dare intend this?
Did you know one day I'd come to you
And search of your forgiveness?

Is it true I'm your heartbeat?
And you chose to die than to live without me?
What sacred delight
What infinite wonder
That I'm precious in your sight
You love me like no other, no other
Oh, sacred delight.

Susan McGeown

__Clay & Water__[11]

I like the contrast of the world spinning around so fast and the slow progression of becoming who I am becoming. All in God's time. Amen!

These days are passing over me
At the speed of light
And standing here in their shadows
I'm silenced at the sight
Like water on the wind I sense the change to come
All that I've held in like teardrops run

I am clay and I am water
Falling forward in this order
While the world spins 'round so fast
Slowly I'm becoming who I am

Nothing ever stays the same
The wheel will always turn
I feel the fire in the change
But somehow it doesn't burn
Like a beggar blessed I stumble in the Grace
Reaching out my hand for what awaits

I am clay and I am water
Falling forward in this order
While the world spins 'round so fast
Slowly I'm becoming who I am

I will live
From my heart
And I will catch the lines of love as they come
Back to You
I know they'll lead
And into You
I know I'll lean

12

Blest Be The Tie That Binds[12]

This is an old Baptist hymn. My memories are as a child, standing with a congregation of believers in a circle holding hands and singing it as someone was leaving. I only know the first verse by heart, but what a hopeful, powerful meaning it carries.

Blest be the tie that binds, Our hearts in Christian love;
The fellowship of kindred minds, Is like to that above.

Before our Father's throne, We pour our ardent prayers;
Our fears, our hopes, our aims are one, Our comforts, and our cares.

We share our mutual woes, Our mutual burdens bear;
And often for each other flows, The sympathizing tear.

When we asunder part, It gives us inward pain;
But we shall still be joined in heart, And hope to meet again.

Faithful to Me[13]

*This song is sung a cappella (without musical accompaniment).
If I was allowed one song to be able to sing, it would probably be this one.*

All the chisels I've dulled carving idols of stone
That have crumbled like sand beneath the waves
I've recklessly built all my dreams in the sand
Just to watch them wash away
Through another day, another trial, another chance to reconcile
To One who sees past all I see
Reaching out my weary hand, I pray that You'd understand
You're the only One Who's faithful to me
All the pennies I've wasted in my wishing well
I have thrown like stones to the sea
I have cast my lots, dropped my guard, searched aimlessly
For a faith to be faithful to me
Through another day, another trial, another chance to reconcile
To One Who sees past all I see
Reaching out my weary hand, I pray that You'd understand
You're the only One Who's faithful to me

Susan McGeown

<u>Valley's Fill First</u>[14]

Many know that I struggle with depression.
This song is particularly near and dear to my heart, possibly because of that.
It's a hopeful, joyful, powerful anthem for me because of the vivid truth of it:
"Down in the valley it seems that I'm at my worst. My consolation is that You baptized
this earth and down in the valley, Valleys fill first."

This is a valley, That I'm walking through
And it feels like forever, Since I've been close to you
My friends up above me, Don't understand why I struggle like I do
My shadow's my only, only companion, And at night he leaves, too

Down in the valley, Dying of thirst
Down in the valley, It seems that I'm at my worst
My consolation is that, You baptized this earth
Well, down in the valley, Valleys fill first

Out in this wasteland, I miss the mountaintop view
But it's here in this valley, That I'm surrounded by You
Though I'm not here by my will, It's where Your view is most clear
So I stay in this valley, If it takes 40 years

Down in the valley, Dying of thirst
When I'm down in the valley, It seems that I'm at my worst
My consolation is that, You baptized this earth,
Well, down in the valley, Valleys fill first

And it's like that long Saturday,
Between Your death and the rising day
When no one wrote a word, Wondered is this the end

But You were down there in the well, Saving those that fell
Bringing them to the mountain again
Oh, I'm down in the valley, Dying of thirst
When I'm down in the valley, It seems that I'm at my worst
My consolation is that, You baptized this earth
Well, down in the valley, Valleys fill first

14

SONGS

Brave[15]

Status Quo: the existing state of affairs. Is that what you want?

The gate is wide, The road is paved in moderation
The crowd is kind and quick to pull you in
Welcome to the middle ground
You're safe and sound and Until now it's where I've been

'Cause it's been fear that ties me down to everything
But it's been love, Your love, that cuts the strings
So long status quo, I think I just let go
You make me want to be brave
The way it always was, Is no longer good enough
You make me want to be brave

I am small, And I speak when I'm spoken to
But I am willing to risk it all
I say Your name, Just Your name and I'm ready to jump
Even ready to fall.

Why did I take this vow of compromise?
Why did I try to keep it all inside?
So long status quo, I think I just let go
You make me want to be brave
The way it always was, Is no longer good enough
You make me want to be brave

I've never known a fire that didn't begin with a flame
Every storm will start with just a drop of rain
But if you believe in me, That changes everything
So long, I'm gone, So long status quo, I think I just let go
You make me want to be brave, I wanna be brave
The way it always was , Is no longer good enough
You make me want to be brave

15

Faith Enough[16]

This song takes a bit of thinking about to appreciate.
It's inspired by the Ernest Hemingway quote pictured on this page.
Can you appreciate the song's meaning?

> The world breaks everyone
> and afterward many are strong
> at the broken places.
>
> – Ernest Hemingway,
>   A Farewell to Arms

The ice is thin enough for walkin'
The rope is worn enough to climb
My throat is dry enough for talkin'
The world is crumbling but I know why
The world is crumbling but I know why

The storm is wild enough for sailing
The bridge is weak enough to cross
This body frail enough for fighting
I'm home enough to know I'm lost
Home enough to know I'm lost

It's just enough to be strong
In the broken places, in the broken places
It's just enough to be strong
Should the world rely on faith tonight

(continued)

(continued)

The land unfit enough for planting
Barren enough to conceive
Poor enough to gain the treasure
Enough a cynic to believe, Enough a cynic to believe
It's just enough to be strong
In the broken places, in the broken places
It's just enough to be strong
Should the world rely on faith tonight

Confused enough to know direction
The sun eclipsed enough to shine
Be still enough to finally tremble
And see enough to know I'm blind
And see enough to know I'm blind

It's just enough to be strong
In the broken places, in the broken places
It's just enough to be strong
Should the world rely on faith tonight

It's just enough to be strong
In the broken places, in the broken places
It's just enough to be strong
Should the world rely on faith tonight

Should the world rely on faith tonight
Should the world rely on faith tonight
Tonight, tonight, tonight
Tonight
Tonight

SCRIPTURE

James 5:16b

The earnest prayer of a righteous person has great power and produces wonderful results.

James 5:16

Here is my super power guarantee.

Psalm 63:1-8[17]

O God, you are my God;
I earnestly search for you.
My soul thirsts for you;
my whole body longs for you
in this parched and weary land
where there is no water.
[2] I have seen you in your sanctuary
and gazed upon your power and glory.
[3] Your unfailing love is better than life itself;
how I praise you!
[4] I will praise you as long as I live,
lifting up my hands to you in prayer.
[5] You satisfy me more than the richest feast.
I will praise you with songs of joy.
[6] I lie awake thinking of you,
meditating on you through the night.
[7] Because you are my helper,
I sing for joy in the shadow of your wings.
[8] I cling to you;
your strong right hand holds me securely.

It took me 18 months, but I memorized this entire thing. I couldn't not.

Jeremiah 17:7-8

"But blessed are those who trust in the LORD
and have made the LORD their hope and confidence.
[8] They are like trees planted along a riverbank,
with roots that reach deep into the water.
Such trees are not bothered by the heat
or worried by long months of drought.
Their leaves stay green,
and they never stop producing fruit.

Your roots are as important as your green leaves. Never forget that.

Ephesians 3:14-21

[14] When I think of all this, I fall to my knees and pray to the Father [15] the Creator of everything in heaven and on earth. [16] I pray that from his glorious, unlimited resources he will empower you with inner strength through his Spirit. [17] Then Christ will make his home in your hearts as you trust in him. Your roots will grow down into God's love and keep you strong. [18] And may you have the power to understand, as all God's people should, how wide, how long, how high, and how deep his love is. [19] May you experience the love of Christ, though it is too great to understand fully. Then you will be made complete with all the fullness of life and power that comes from God.
[20] Now all glory to God, who is able, through his mighty power at work within us, to accomplish infinitely more than we might ask or think. [21] Glory to him in the church and in Christ Jesus through all generations forever and ever! Amen.

Another one I spent over a year memorizing. That promise, "to accomplish infinitely more than we might ask or think" is mind blowing to me.
(Because I can think of A LOT of stuff!!)

Romans 8:28

And we know that God causes everything to work together for the good of those who love God and are called according to his purpose for them.

This shows up in almost every one of my women's conferences. My favorite word in this verse is "everything." There's something incredibly freeing, incredibly empowering with the knowledge that everything - not just the good stuff - will work together for good. What could possibly go wrong with that promise?

Exodus 33:13a

Show me Your intentions so I will understand You more fully and do exactly what You want me to do.

"Paint a Big Black Arrow, Lord, and I'll happily follow it."

Jeremiah 29:11

"For I know the plans I have for you," says the Lord. "They are plans for good and not for disaster, to you a future and a hope."

I have this engraved on a silver bracelet. What a promise!

Proverbs 31:10-31

[10] Who can find a virtuous and capable wife?
She is more precious than rubies.
[11] Her husband can trust her, and she will greatly enrich his life.
[12] She brings him good, not harm, all the days of her life.
[13] She finds wool and flax and busily spins it.
[14] She is like a merchant's ship, bringing her food from afar.
[15] She gets up before dawn to prepare breakfast for her household
and plan the day's work for her servant girls.
[16] She goes to inspect a field and buys it;
with her earnings she plants a vineyard.
[17] She is energetic and strong, a hard worker.
[18] She makes sure her dealings are profitable;
her lamp burns late into the night.
[19] Her hands are busy spinning thread, her fingers twisting fiber.
[20] She extends a helping hand to the poor
and opens her arms to the needy.
[21] She has no fear of winter for her household,
for everyone has warm clothes.
[22] She makes her own bedspreads.
She dresses in fine linen and purple gowns.
[23] Her husband is well known at the city gates,
where he sits with the other civic leaders.
[24] She makes belted linen garments
and sashes to sell to the merchants.
[25] She is clothed with strength and dignity,
and she laughs without fear of the future.
(continued)

(continued)

²⁶ When she speaks, her words are wise,
and she gives instructions with kindness.
²⁷ She carefully watches everything in her household
and suffers nothing from laziness.
²⁸ Her children stand and bless her. Her husband praises her:
²⁹ "There are many virtuous and capable women in the world,
but you surpass them all!"
³⁰ Charm is deceptive, and beauty does not last;
but a woman who fears the LORD will be greatly praised.
³¹ Reward her for all she has done.
Let her deeds publicly declare her praise.

This is a woman who has made the most of the gifts, talents, blessings, and opportunities that God has given her. I am determined to be that woman, too. How about you?

Matthew 6:21

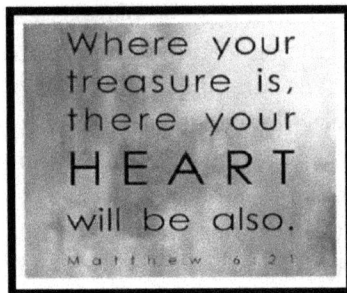

Where your treasure is, there your HEART will be also.

Matthew 6:21

What (or Who) is most precious to your heart? Your answer is eternally important.

Philippians 1:20-21

I eagerly expect and hope that I will in no way be ashamed, but will have sufficient courage so that now as always Christ will be exalted in my body, whether by life or by death. ²¹ For to me, to live is Christ and to die is gain. (NIV)

*I memorized these two verses on a trip to visit family in England.
It is my signature verse and the force behind everything I do.*

22

<u>Amos 3:3</u>

Can two people walk together
without agreeing on the direction?

While this verse references two people, for me it is a reminder that if I want God's help, blessing, and smile I need to travel in the same direction that He is headed and no other.

<u>Jeremiah 33:3</u>

Ask me and I will tell you remarkable secrets you do not know about things to come.

I found this verse early on in my life. There was something really wonderful about the promise of secrets being told to just me ...

<u>Matthew 6:27</u>

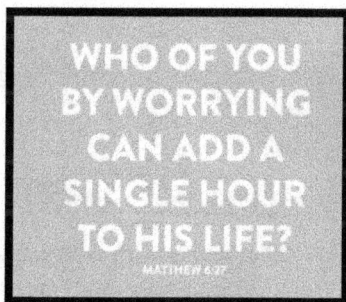

WHO OF YOU
BY WORRYING
CAN ADD A
SINGLE HOUR
TO HIS LIFE?
MATTHEW 6:27

*How much time have
you lost worrying?*

<u>Romans 10:9-10</u>

[9] If you openly declare that Jesus is Lord and believe in your heart that God raised him from the dead, you will be saved. [10] For it is by believing in your heart that you are made right with God, and it is by openly declaring your faith that you are saved.

Here it is: the how and the why of salvation.

23

Isaiah 41:10

Don't be afraid, for I am with you.
Don't be discouraged, for I am your God.
I will strengthen you and help you.
I will hold you up with my victorious right hand.

Don't. Seriously, don't.
He will. He does.
His promises never fail.

Numbers 6:24-26

[24] 'May the LORD bless you
and protect you.
[25] May the LORD smile on you
and be gracious to you.
[26] May the LORD show you his favor
and give you his peace.'

Just imagine, if you can, God looking directly at you and you causing Him to smile.
Just imagine…

Romans 8:38-39

And I am convinced that nothing can ever separate us from God's love. Neither death nor life, neither angels nor demons, neither our fears for today nor our worries about tomorrow—not even the powers of hell can separate us from God's love. [39] No power in the sky above or in the earth below—indeed, nothing in all creation will ever be able to separate us from the love of God that is revealed in Christ Jesus our Lord.

I love this verse because so many of the things on the "neither list"
regularly creep onto my "worry list"…

Proverbs 19:21

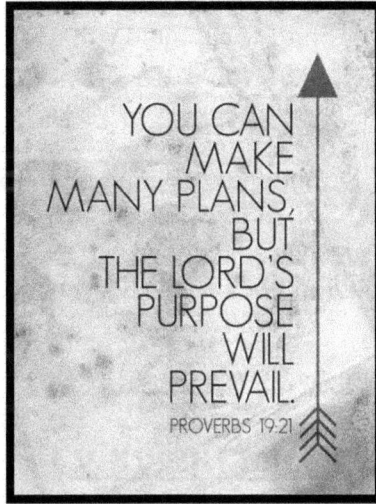

YOU CAN
MAKE
MANY PLANS,
BUT
THE LORD'S
PURPOSE
WILL
PREVAIL.
PROVERBS 19:21

*In case you think
you are in charge of anything.
Always remember Who's The Boss.*

Psalm 23:4

Yea, though I walk through the valley of the shadow of death,
I will fear no evil: for thou art with me
(KJV)

*I remind myself of this promise regularly;
especially when things are looking particularly dicey.*

John 17:20

"I am praying not only for these disciples but also for all who will
ever believe in me through their message."

*This is Jesus.
Praying, in the Garden of Gethsemane,
specifically for you.*

John 14:27

I am leaving you with a gift – peace of mind and heart.
The Friend, the Holy Spirit will remind you of all the things I have
told you.
I am leaving you well and whole.
That's my parting gift to you: Peace.
It is a gift the world cannot give. I don't leave you the way you're
used to being left –
feeling abandoned, bereft.
So don't be troubled or afraid.
(NLT & MSG)

What a present. Thank You, Lord.

Psalm 139:23-24

[23] Search me, O God, and know my heart;
test me and know my anxious thoughts.
[24] Point out anything in me that offends you,
and lead me along the path of everlasting life.

What benefit is it to be aware of my anxious thoughts?
What good is it to test me and show me my weaknesses?
See the below verse …

2 Corinthians 12:9a

"My grace is enough; it's all you need.
My strength comes into its own in your weakness."
(MSG)

Do you appreciate the magnitude of this promise?
Your greatest weakness …
is what God wants to make your greatest strength.
W.O.W.

3 John 4

I could have no greater joy than to hear
that my children are following the truth.

Guess what my #1 prayer request is?

Revelations 21:4

He will wipe every tear from their eyes, and
there will be no more death or sorrow or crying or pain.
All these things are gone forever.

Gone. F.O.R.E.V.E.R.

Philippians 3:13-14

Forgetting the past and looking forward to what lies ahead, I press on
to reach the end of the race and receive the heavenly prize for which
God, through Christ Jesus, is calling us.

*I love that "forgetting" part most of all. There's a saying I like that must be inspired by
this: "Don't look back, you're not going that way." Too true!*

Mark 10:27

Jesus looked at them intently and said, "Humanly speaking, it is
impossible. But not with God. Everything is possible with God."

Picture Jesus, looking intently at you and saying this.

Ezekiel 36:26

And I will give you a new heart, and I will put a new spirit in you.
I will take out your stony, stubborn heart and
give you a tender, responsive heart.

I am different now. Thank you, God!

John 3:16-17

[16] For this is how God loved the world: He gave his one and only Son, so that everyone who believes in him will not perish but have eternal life. [17] God sent his Son into the world not to judge the world, but to save the world through him.

Many people know John 3:16 by heart.
John 3:17 is just as precious and just as important.

Romans 12:2

So here's what I want you to do, God helping you:
Take your everyday, ordinary life –
your sleeping, eating, going-to-work, and walking-around life –
and place it before God as an offering.
Let God change the way you think.
Embracing what God does for you
is the best thing you can do for Him.
Then you will learn to know God's will for you,
which is good and pleasing and perfect.
(NLT & MSG)

How to be good, pleasing, and perfect… Okay. I'll be that.

Zephaniah 3:17

"For the LORD your God is living among you.
He is a mighty savior.
He will take delight in you with gladness.
With his love, he will calm all your fears.
He will rejoice over you with joyful songs."

I want God to take delight in me. Don't you?

Matthew 28:18-20

Jesus came and told his disciples, "I have been given all authority in heaven and on earth. [19] Therefore, go and make disciples of all the nations, baptizing them in the name of the Father and the Son and the Holy Spirit. [20] Teach these new disciples to obey all the commands I have given you. And be sure of this: I am with you always, even to the end of the age."

Here is another reminder of my superpower. (In case you are still wondering.)

John 14:6

Jesus said, "I am the way, the truth, and the life. No one can come to the Father except through me."

No. One.
It's the reason Jesus came.

I Thessalonians 5:16-18

Be cheerful no matter what;
pray all the time;
thank God no matter what happens.
This is the way God wants you who belong to Christ Jesus to live.
(MSG)

"Be cheerful, no matter what." How can that be? That's because God is timeless. Read and smile over the verse below, which says it best.

Deuteronomy 31:8a

Do not be afraid or discouraged,
for the Lord will personally go ahead of you.

Isn't that a perfect reason to be cheerful (and fearless) regardless of your circumstances?

SCRIPTURE

Zechariah 9:12

I am a prisoner of hope.

What a delightful prison.

2 Timothy 1:7

For God has not given us a spirit of fear and timidity, but of power, love, and self-discipline.

Over thirty years ago, a minister had us as a congregation, repeat this verse over and over again in the hopes that we would write it on our heart. I did.

Hebrews 11:1

It's so true. Things done in faith only ever make sense from the worldly perspective when viewed in reverse.

Luke 12:12

The Holy Spirit will tell you at that very moment what you must say.
(CEB)

Phew, that's a relief.

Psalm 84:11

For the LORD God is a sun and shield;
the LORD bestows favor and honor.
No good thing does he withhold
from those who walk uprightly. (ESV)

No good thing. NO. GOOD. THING. (And remember, He knows best.)

Ecclesiastes 3:1-11

For everything there is a season,
a time for every activity under heaven.
[2] A time to be born and a time to die.
A time to plant and a time to harvest.
[3] A time to kill and a time to heal.
A time to tear down and a time to build up.
[4] A time to cry and a time to laugh.
A time to grieve and a time to dance.
[5] A time to scatter stones and a time to gather stones.
A time to embrace and a time to turn away.
[6] A time to search and a time to quit searching.
A time to keep and a time to throw away.
[7] A time to tear and a time to mend.
A time to be quiet and a time to speak.
[8] A time to love and a time to hate.
A time for war and a time for peace.
[9] What do people really get for all their hard work? [10] I have seen the burden God has placed on us all. [11] Yet God has made everything beautiful for its own time. He has planted eternity in the human heart, but even so, people cannot see the whole scope of God's work from beginning to end.

These verses are a writer's description of real life and reminds us of God's authority over all of it. It recognizes the hard parts of life, but also promises a rainbow after the storm. Always.

Psalm 30:4-5

Sing to the LORD, all you godly ones!
Praise his holy name.
[5] For his anger lasts only a moment,
but his favor lasts a lifetime!
Weeping may last through the night,
but joy comes with the morning.

Joy in the morning. Yes, Lord!!

Isaiah 6:8

Then I heard the Lord asking,
"Whom shall I send as a messenger to these people?
Who will go for us?" and I said, "Here I am! Send me!"

Have you ever said that? "Here I am, Lord! Send me!"

I Thessalonians 5:5-8

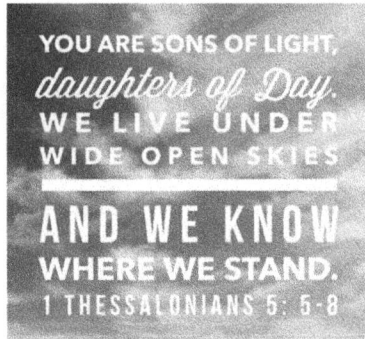

YOU ARE SONS OF LIGHT,
daughters of Day.
WE LIVE UNDER
WIDE OPEN SKIES
AND WE KNOW
WHERE WE STAND.
1 THESSALONIANS 5: 5-8

Are you a daughter of the day?

Matthew 25:21

Well done my good and faithful servant. You have been faithful in
handling this small amount, so now I will give you many more
responsibilities.

Oh, to be told this…

<u>**2 Thessalonians 2:16-17**</u>

Now may our Lord Jesus Christ himself and God our Father, who loved us and by his grace gave us eternal comfort and a wonderful hope, comfort you and strengthen you in every good thing you do and say.

2 Thessalonians 2:16-17

I wish this for you all.

QUOTATIONS

Sometimes your only available transportation is a leap of faith.

Margaret Shepard

Oswald Chambers[18]

I remember (trying) to read Oswald Chambers' book <u>My Utmost For His Highest</u> for the first time when I was in my early 20's. It didn't come easy. Yet I discovered that if I read the short daily entry more than once (more than twice sometimes) I'd often get hit with a spiritual truth that was so incredibly powerful, I'd be compelled to copy it down in my thoughts journal. So I persisted. The profound collection of outstanding spiritual truths (only some of which are listed below) was life changing.

If you are depending upon anything but Him, you will never know when He is gone.

Leave Him to be the source of all your dreams and joys and delights and go out and obey what He said.

The love of God pays no attention to the distinctions made by natural individuality.

My worth to God in public is what I am in private.

Faith is not intelligent understanding; faith is deliberate commitment to a Person where I see no way.

Obey Him with glad, reckless joy.

Take care lest you play the hypocrite by spending all your time trying to get others right before you worship God yourself.

The proof that we are rightly related to God is that we do our best whether we feel inspired or not.

Certainty is the mark of a common-sense life; gracious uncertainty is the mark of the spiritual life.

Faith is the heroic effort of your life.

We are in danger of forgetting that we cannot do what God does and that God will not do what we can do.

35

God does not keep a person immune from trouble. He says, "I will
be with you in trouble."

The great enemy of the life of faith in God is not sin, but the good
which is not good enough.

You can never give another person that which you have found, but
you can make him homesick for what you have.

God never gives strength for tomorrow, or for the next hour, but
only for the strain of the minute.

Get into the habit of dealing with God about everything.

God rarely allows a soul to see how great a blessing he or she is.

It is not so true that "prayer changes things" as that prayer changes
me and I change things.

Faith must be tested, because it can be turned into a personal
possession only through conflict.

The life that is rightly related to God is as natural as breathing
wherever it goes. The lives that have been of most blessing to you
are those who were unconscious of it.

Crises always reveal character.

The great need is not to *do* things but to *believe* things.

God will never reveal more truth about Himself until you have
obeyed what you know already.

Prayer does not fit us for the greater works; prayer *is* the greater work.

We have to be exceptional in ordinary things.

All God's people are ordinary people made extraordinary by the matter He has given them.

When I stand face to face with God I will discover that through my obedience thousands were blessed.

Jesus hates the wrong in man, and Calvary is the estimate of His hatred.

Refuse to be swamped by the cares of this life.

You have to walk in the light of the vision that has been given to you and not compare yourself with others or judge them, that is between them and God.

God is the God of our yesterdays and He allows the memory of them in order to turn the past into a ministry of spiritual culture for the future.

God will garrison where we have failed to.

Leave the broken, irreversible past in God's hands and step out into the invincible future with Him. Resolutely slam and lock the door on past sin and failure and throw away the key.

"Faith is deliberate confidence in the character of God whose ways you may not understand at the time."

Oswald Chambers

C. S. Lewis[19]

My faithful Bible study friends know how much I love C.S. Lewis. I love him so much that I taught his outstanding book, Mere Christianity, using pictures. The title 'Mere Christianity' is actually a play on words. Christianity is anything but small or 'mere', however, C.S. does an outstanding job trying to take the deep, abstract concepts and make them ... simple. Sorta.

God doesn't judge man on his raw material at all, but on what he has done with it.

Good people know about both good and evil; bad people do not know about either.

A proud person is always looking down on things and people, and, of course, as long as you are looking down, you cannot see something that is above you.

All that is not eternal is eternally useless.[20]

God whispers to us in our pleasures, speaks in our conscience, but shouts in our pain.

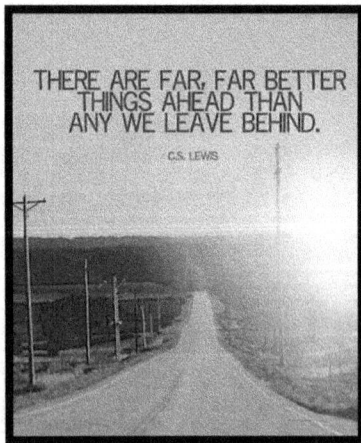

THERE ARE FAR, FAR BETTER THINGS AHEAD THAN ANY WE LEAVE BEHIND.

C.S. LEWIS

38

<u>Mother Teresa</u>[21]

Mother Theresa is the epitome of the might and power that can be bestowed on any human being, regardless of worldly circumstances, by the Holy Spirit working within us.

I know God will not give me anything I can't handle. I just wish that He didn't trust me so much.

Peace begins with a smile.

Loneliness and the feeling of being unwanted is the most terrible poverty.

Be faithful in small things because it is in them that your strength lies.

The miracle is not that we do this work, but that we are happy to do it.

Make us worthy, Lord, to serve others throughout the world
who live and die in poverty or hunger.
Give them, through our hands, this day their daily bread,
and by our understanding love, give peace and joy.

God works best through nothing.

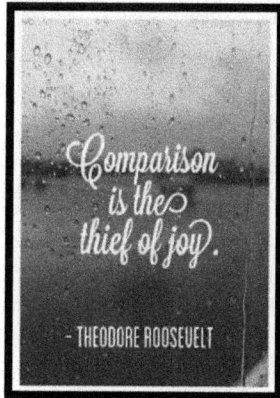

Comparison is the thief of joy.

- THEODORE ROOSEVELT

AMEN, Teddy.
A.M.E.N.

Rick Warren[22]

Rich Warren's book, The Purpose Driven Life, is a book every believer should read. It is easy to read, practical and profound.

You can't claim to be good if you've never been tempted to be bad. You can't claim to be faithful, if you've never had the opportunity to be unfaithful.

God never does anything accidentally, and He never makes mistakes.

There is no growth without change, no change without fear or loss, and no loss without pain.

Your identity is in eternity, and your homeland is heaven.

You were not put on this earth to be remembered. You were put here to prepare for eternity.

Abraham was old, Jacob was insecure, Leah was unattractive, Joseph was abused, Moses stuttered, Gideon was poor, Samson was codependent, Rahab was immoral, David had affairs and all kinds of family problems, Elijah was suicidal, Jeremiah was depressed, Jonah was reluctant, Naomi was a widow, John the Baptist was eccentric to say the least, Peter was impulsive and hot tempered, Martha worried a lot, the Samaritan woman had several failed marriages, Zacchaeus was unpopular, Thomas had doubts, Paul had poor health, and Timothy was timid. What excuse have you been using?

When you live in the light of eternity your values change.

The more God give you the more responsible He expects you to be.

You are as close to God as you choose to be.

Your character is essentially the sum of your habits.

God is far more interested in what you are than what you do.

> # The smile of God is the goal of your life.
> Rick Warren

Elisabeth Elliot[23]

Elizabeth Elliot: missionary, speaker, author.

There is nothing worth living for, unless it is worth dying for.

Don't dig up in doubt what you planted in faith.

If you believe in a God who controls the big things, you have to believe in a God who controls the little things.

You are loved with an everlasting love. And underneath are the everlasting arms.

The fact that I'm a woman doesn't make me a different kind of Christian, but the fact that I'm a Christian does make me a different kind of woman.

When you don't know what to do next, just do the thing in front of you.

41

Corrie Ten Boom[24]

She was a Christian during the time of the Holocaust. Her story is incredible.

You can never learn that Christ is all you need, until Christ is all you have.

If the Devil cannot make us bad, he will make us busy.

Don't bother to give God instructions, just report for duty.

Is prayer your steering wheel or your spare tire?

In darkness God's truth shines most clear.

The measure of a life, after all, is not its duration, but its donation.

Worry is like a rocking chair; it keeps you moving but doesn't get you anywhere.

Never be afraid to trust an unknown future to a known God.

When I try, I fail. When I trust, He succeeds.

Worry doesn't empty tomorrow of its sorrow. It empties today of its strength.

ROCK
BOTTOM
HAS BUILT
MORE
HEROES
THAN
PRIVILEGE

A. W. Tozer[25]

A. W. Tozer's The Pursuit of God *offers a profound insight into God and our relationship with God. Reading it will make you a better believer. Honest.*

There is an unseen Deity present, a knowing, feeling Personality, and He is indivisible from the Father and the Son, so that if you were to be suddenly transferred to heaven itself you wouldn't be any closer to God than you are now, for God is already here.

They have seen heaven draw nearer and earth recede; the things of this world have become less and less attractive, and the things of heaven have begun to pull and pull as the moon pulls at the sea…

The heart that knows God, can find God anywhere.

If there is true faith within, there will be obedience to God without.

The person who has met God in a living encounter can know the joy of worshipping Him, whether in the silences of life or in the storms of life.

It is not that I plant, but what I plant that matters.

Since a believer is part of God's eternal purpose, he knows he must win at last, and he can afford to be calm even when the battle seems to be temporarily going against him. The world has no such "blissful center" upon which to rest.

An open mind to be taught. A tender heart to believe. A surrendered will to obey.

Each of the fruits of the Spirit is but a phase of love. Joy is love exulting, peace is love reposing, patience is love enduring, goodness is the good manners of love; kindness is love in action; faithfulness is love confiding; gentleness is love yielding; and self-control is true self-love.

Susan McGeown

Anyone can do the possible; add a bit of courage and zeal and some may do the phenomenal; only Christians are obliged to do the impossible.

The world must see the light of heaven in our faces if it would believe in the reality of our religion.

The genuine Christian should be a walking mystery because he surely is a walking miracle.

God cannot fill what hasn't been emptied.

Faith is the gaze of a soul upon a saving God.

In myself, nothing; in God, everything.

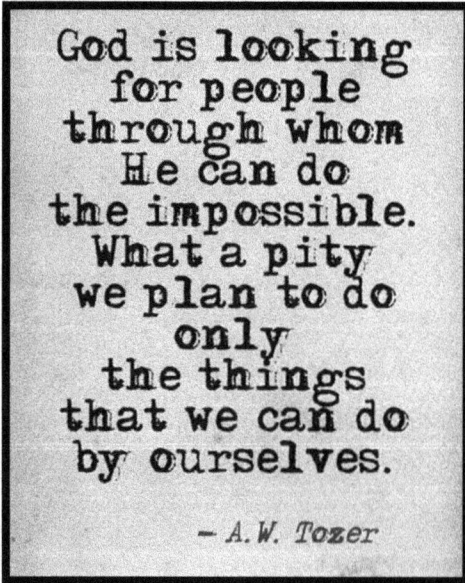

> God is looking
> for people
> through whom
> He can do
> the impossible.
> What a pity
> we plan to do
> only
> the things
> that we can do
> by ourselves.
>
> – A.W. Tozer

Let every man abide in the calling wherein he is called and his work will be as sacred as the work of the ministry. It is not what a man does that determines whether his work is sacred or secular; it is why he does it.

The great of the kingdom have been those who loved God more than others did.

We must offer all our acts to God and believe that He accepts them. We must not accept one another's notions, copy on another's lives, and make one another's experiences the model for our own.

Let us believe that God is in all our simple deeds and learn to find Him there.

If my fire is not large it is yet real, and many be those who can light their candle at its flame.
(A. W. Tozer)

45

Jennifer LeClaire[26]

My newest study has been regarding the Holy Spirit. I found the book Mornings With The Holy Spirit by Jennifer LeClaire at our local book store and have thoroughly enjoyed this devotional and it's profound prospective about the Trinity and us. I can't recommend it highly enough.

Quicken my heart to walk with You and talk with You throughout the day so I don't miss anything You are trying to reveal to me.

Give me the strength and courage to follow through on difficult decisions, especially when it comes to those closest to me. I want to please You more than people.

Please break in with Your perspective on things I'm not seeing clearly.

Things that bother you don't bother Me because I see the solution. I see the growth possibility for you. I see the opportunity for you to learn more about Christ.

Help me to learn quickly what You are trying to teach me.

"I want it to be obvious to everyone around me that I have been in Your presence by the fruit that manifests in my life."

LeClaire

46

Philip Yancey[27]

I read Philip Yancey's book <u>Prayer: Does It Make Any Difference?</u> at first reluctantly. What a blessing it turned out to be. It transformed my prayer life magnificently.

Prayer is a subversive act performed in a world that constantly calls faith into question.

The main purpose of prayer is not to make life easier, nor to gain magical powers, but to know God. I need God more than anything I might get from God.

> *"I have learned that faith means trusting in advance what will only make sense in reverse."*
>
> *Philip Yancey*

We do not pray to tell God what He does not know, nor to remind Him of things He has forgotten. He already cares for the things we pray about … He has simply been waiting for us to care about them with Him. When we pray, we stand by God and look with Him toward those people and problems.

I remind myself that the Son of God, who had spoken worlds into being and sustains all that exists, felt a compelling need to pray. He prayed as if it made a difference, as if the time He devoted to prayer mattered every bit as much as the time he devoted to caring for people.

47

Jesus knew the sensation of getting no answer to his pleas.

If God doesn't want something for me, I shouldn't want it either…Nothing lies beyond the reach of prayer except that which lies outside the will of God.

God, show me what You are doing today and how I can be a part of it.

The habit of not praying is far more difficult to break than the habit of praying.

Finite humans can never know the will of an infinite God with absolute certainty.

Maybe we can see things through tears that we can't see dry-eyed.

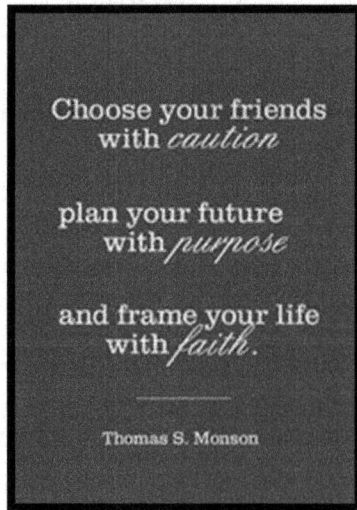

Choose your friends
with *caution*

plan your future
with *purpose*

and frame your life
with *faith*.

Thomas S. Monson

<u>Timothy Keller</u>[28]

The first book I read by Timothy Keller was <u>The Prodigal God</u> an outstanding, insightful, amazing discussion on Jesus' parable about the prodigal son. I guarantee if you read it, your mind will be blown. As a result, I purchased and read Keller's book, <u>The Reason For God</u> which resulted in a year long study in both my Bible study groups. Yes, it was that good.

Forgiveness must be granted before it can be felt.

The pattern of the Cross means that the world's glorification of power, might, and status is exposed and defeated. On the Cross, Christ wins through losing, triumphs through defeat, achieves power through weakness and service, comes to wealth via giving everything all away. Jesus Christ turns the values of the world upside down.

Strong faith in a weak branch is fatally inferior to weak faith in a strong branch.

It is therefore important to consider the Bible's core claims about who Jesus is and whether He rose from the dead before you reject it for its less central and more controversial teachings.

Sin is seeking to become oneself, to get an identity, apart from God.

courage does not always roar.

sometimes courage is the quiet voice

at the end of the day saying,

"i will try again tomorrow"

(mary anne radmacher)

49

The Prayer of St. Patrick[29]

Originally attributed to St. Patrick,
the author of this beautiful prayer is now thought to be anonymous.
Whoever wrote it, what a perfect prayer to start each day!

I arise today, Through the strength of heaven;
Light of the sun, Splendor of fire,
Speed of lightning, Swiftness of the wind,
Depth of the sea, Stability of the earth,
Firmness of the rock.

I arise today, Through God's strength to pilot me;
God's might to uphold me, God's wisdom to guide me,
God's eye to look before me, God's ear to hear me,
God's word to speak for me, God's hand to guard me,
God's way to lie before me, God's shield to protect me,
God's hosts to save me
Afar and anear, Alone or in a multitude.

Christ shield me today, Against wounding
Christ with me, Christ before me, Christ behind me,
Christ in me, Christ beneath me, Christ above me,
Christ on my right, Christ on my left,
Christ when I lie down, Christ when I sit down,
Christ in the heart of everyone who thinks of me,
Christ in the mouth of everyone who speaks of me,
Christ in the eye that sees me,
Christ in the ear that hears me.

I arise today,
Through the mighty strength
Of the Lord of creation.

<u>**Desiderata by Max Erhmann**</u>[30]

I read this for the first time when I was in my teens. For shy little, quiet little Susan, it was a gentle yet powerful admonition to seriously work toward discovering the person I knew God wanted me to be.

Go placidly amid the noise and haste,
and remember what peace there may be in silence.
As far as possible without surrender
be on good terms with all persons.
Speak your truth quietly and clearly;
and listen to others,
even the dull and the ignorant;
they too have their story.
Avoid loud and aggressive persons,
they are vexations to the spirit.
If you compare yourself with others,
you may become vain and bitter;
for always there will be greater and lesser persons than yourself.
Enjoy your achievements as well as your plans.
Keep interested in your own career, however humble;
it is a real possession in the changing fortunes of time.
Exercise caution in your business affairs;
for the world is full of trickery.
But let this not blind you to what virtue there is;
many persons strive for high ideals;
and everywhere life is full of heroism.
Be yourself.
Especially, do not feign affection.
Neither be cynical about love;
for in the face of all aridity and disenchantment
it is as perennial as the grass.
Take kindly the counsel of the years,
gracefully surrendering the things of youth.
Nurture strength of spirit to shield you in sudden misfortune.

(continued)

(continued)

But do not distress yourself with dark imaginings.
Many fears are born of fatigue and loneliness.
Beyond a wholesome discipline,
be gentle with yourself.
You are a child of the universe,
no less than the trees and the stars;
you have a right to be here.
And whether or not it is clear to you,
no doubt the universe is unfolding as it should.
Therefore be at peace with God,
whatever you conceive Him to be,
and whatever your labors and aspirations,
in the noisy confusion of life keep peace with your soul.
With all its sham, drudgery, and broken dreams,
it is still a beautiful world.
Be cheerful.
Strive to be happy.

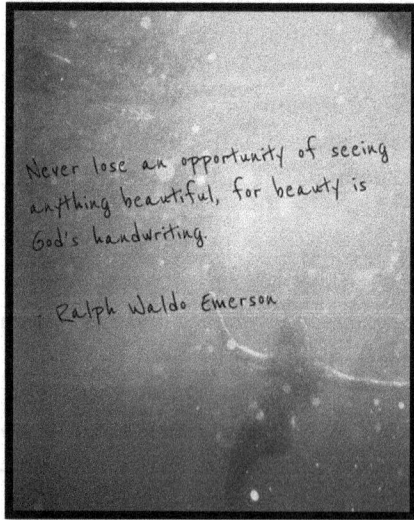

Never lose an opportunity of seeing
anything beautiful, for beauty is
God's handwriting.

— Ralph Waldo Emerson

QUOTATIONS

I Make The Effort by Ram Dass

Do you make the effort?

I make the effort
to maintain a ground of oceanic silence
out of which arises the multitude of phenomena of daily life.

I make the effort
to see and to passionately open in love
to the Spirit that infuses all things.

I make the effort
to see the Beloved in everyone
and to serve the Beloved through everyone
(including the earth).

I often fail in these aspirations
because I lose the balance between separateness and unity,
get lost in my separateness,
and feel afraid.

But I make the effort.

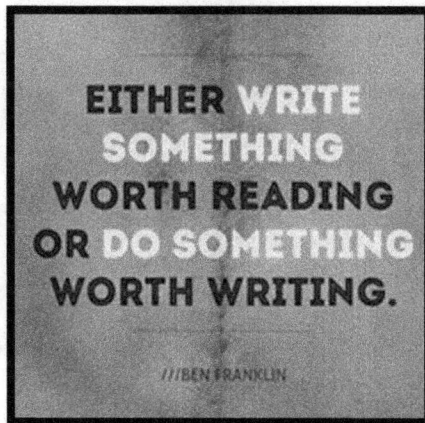

EITHER WRITE SOMETHING WORTH READING OR DO SOMETHING WORTH WRITING.

///BEN FRANKLIN

53

Empower Me[31] by Ted Loder

Empower me
to be a bold participant rather than a timid saint in waiting,
in the difficult ordinariness of now.

To exercise the authority of honesty;
Rather than to defer to power,
Or deceive to get it.

To influence someone for justice,
Rather than impress anyone for gain.

And, by grace, to find treasures of joy, of friendship, of peace
hidden in the fields of the daily,
You give me to plow.

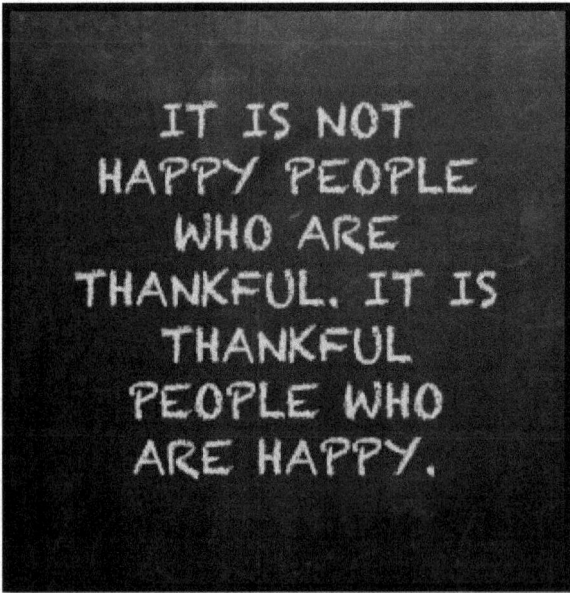

IT IS NOT
HAPPY PEOPLE
WHO ARE
THANKFUL. IT IS
THANKFUL
PEOPLE WHO
ARE HAPPY.

54

John Ortberg[32]

If you want to walk on water, you have to get out of the boat.

You are a piece of work by God.

A calling is something you discover, not something you choose.

Jesus is not finished yet. He is still looking for people who will dare to trust Him.

We are not called just to work <u>for</u> God. We are called to work <u>with</u> God.

So Peter got out of the boat, started walking on the water and came toward Jesus. (Matthew 14:29)
"Peter failed. But I think there were eleven bigger failures sitting in the boat... It was Peter's willingness to risk failure that helped him to grow."

COURAGE
is fear that
has said its
PRAYERS

Dorothy Bernard said this.
Isn't it fabulous?
Isn't it so true?

55

Special Quotes

Here are some favorite quotes from individuals that have inspired me over the years.

Give me such love for God and men as will blot out all hatred and bitterness.
Dietrich Bonhoeffer

The greatest use of life is to spend it for something that will outlast it.
William James

Never doubt in the dark what God told you in the light.
V. Raymond Edman

Why should I ask of Him that He would change for me the course of things? I who ought to love, above all, the order established by His wisdom and maintained by His Providence, shall I wish that order to be dissolved on my account?
Rousseau

When I pray, coincidences happen. When I don't, they don't.
Archbishop William Temple

I am only one; but still I am one. I cannot do everything; but still I can do something; and because I cannot do everything, I will not refuse to do the something that I can do.

Edward Everett Hale

56

Isn't it the greatest possible disaster, when you are wrestling with
God, not to be beaten?
Simone Weil

God is not really silent, we are deaf.
Teresa of Avila

Some of God's greatest gifts are unanswered prayers.
Garth Brooks

Coincidence is a small miracle when
God chooses to remain anonymous
Albert Einstein

A Franciscan Benediction
May God bless you with discomfort
At easy answers, half-truths, and superficial relationship
So that you may live deep within your heart.
May God bless you with anger
At injustice, oppression, and exploitation of people,
So that you may work for justice, freedom and peace.
May God bless you with tears
To shed for those who suffer pain, rejection, hunger, and war,
So that you may reach out your hand to comfort them and
To turn their pain into joy.
And may God bless you with enough foolishness
To believe that you can make a difference in the world,
So that you can do what others claim cannot be done
To bring justice and kindness to all our children and the poor.
Amen.

To know oneself, is above all, to know what one lacks. It is to
measure oneself against the Truth, and not the other way around.
Flannery O'Connor

What lies behind us and what lies before us are tiny matters
compared to what lies within us.
Ralph Waldo Emerson.
Let me use disappointment as material for patience.
Let me use success as material for thankfulness.
Let me use trouble as material for perseverance.
Let me use danger as material for courage.
Let me use reproach as material for long suffering.
Let me use praise as material for humility.
Let me use pleasures as material for temperance.
Let me use pain as material for endurance.
John Baillie

No one can make you feel inferior without your consent.
Eleanor Roosevelt

I live for those who love me,
Whose hearts are kind and true,
For heaven that smiles above me,
And waits my spirit too;
For the cause that lacks assistance,
For the wrong that needs resistance,
For the future in the distance,
And the good that I can do.
George Linnaeus Banks[33]

I am not bound to win, but I am bound to be true.
I am not bound to succeed,
but I am bound to live up to the light I have.
I must stand with anybody that stands right,
stand with him while he is right,
and part with him when he goes wrong.
Abraham Lincoln

QUOTATIONS

In the depth of winter, I finally learned that within me there lay an invincible summer.
Albert Camus

Conduct is what we do; character is what we are.
Conduct is the outward life. Character is the life unseen, hidden within, yet evidenced by that which is seen.
Conduct is external, seen from without; character is internal—operating within.
In the economy of grace, conduct is the offspring of character.
Character is the state of the heart, conduct its outward expression.
Character is the root of the tree, conduct, the fruit it bears.
E.M. Bounds[34]

Do all the good you can,
By all the means you can,
In all the ways you can,
In all the places you can,
To all the people you can,
As long as ever you can.
John Wesley

In faith there is enough light for those who want to believe and enough shadows to blind those who don't."
Blaise Pascal

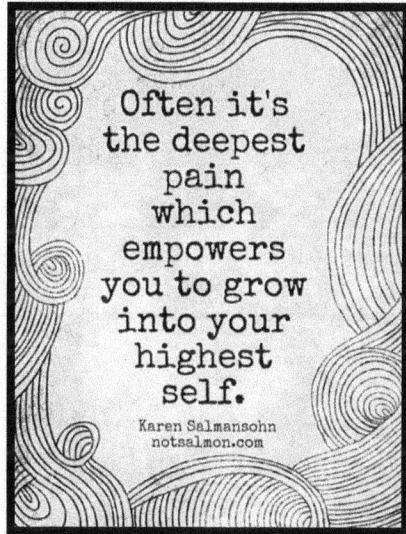

Often it's the deepest pain which empowers you to grow into your highest self.
Karen Salmansohn
notsalmon.com

We are all worms, but I do believe I'm a glow worm.
Winston Churchill

I am only one.
But I am still one.
I cannot do everything,
but still I will not refuse to do the something I can do.
Helen Keller

59

Anonymous Quotes

I wish I knew who to attribute these to. They're fabulous.

Hell is truth seen too late.

Sorrow looks back,
work looks around,
faith looks up.

> Don't let opinions of other people make you doubt about God's plans for you.

Are you a good example or a horrible warning?

He stands best who kneels first.

The tallest kind of preaching is a good example.

Change is inevitable, growth is optional

Whether you think you can or you can't, you're right.

> A
> certain
> darkness
> is
> needed
> to
> see
> the
> stars.

Your attitude is the paintbrush with which you color your life.

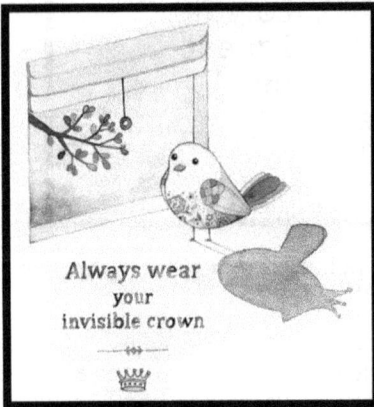

Always wear
your
invisible crown

Lead or follow but don't complain.

Yesterday is history,
tomorrow is a mystery,
but today is a gift;
that's why it's called the present.

Never confuse having a career with having a life.

60

Sue's Favorite Artists & Authors

You can't grow without feeding yourself: read, listen, ask, search, delve, explore, focus, inspect, question … but do it all through prayer and guidance from our precious Holy Spirit. It's the only way it will work. Trust me.

Authors

My Utmost For His Highest, by Oswald Chambers

Mere Christianity, by C. S. Lewis

A Purpose Driven Life, by Rick Warren

The Reason For God, by Tim Keller

The Pursuit of God, by A. W. Tozer

Mornings With The Holy Spirit, by Jennifer LeClair

Prayer, by Philip Yancey

Women of the Bible, by Ann Spangler and Jean Syswerda

Artists

Jennifer Knapp

Amy Grant

Margaret Becker

Jars of Clay

Caedmon's Call

Audio Adrenaline

Susan McGeown

MY NOTES

Write down thoughts, questions, observations, and anything else that comes to mind while you're reading this book!

Words Worth Remembering

Susan McGeown

Words Worth Remembering

Susan McGeown

Words Worth Remembering

Susan McGeown

Words Worth Remembering

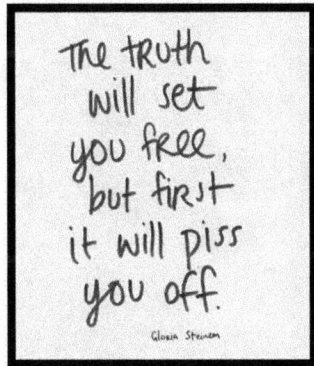

The truth
will set
you free,
but first
it will piss
you off.

Gloria Steinem

About The Author

Susan McGeown is a wife, mother, daughter, sister, friend, aunt, uncle (don't ask), teacher, author … but, most importantly, a "woman after God's own heart." Always working on a new book, she writes historical novels (including *Rosamund's Bower*, 2008 RCRW's Golden Rose winner in the category of 'Novel with Romantic Elements'), contemporary fiction novels, and nonfiction Bible studies.

She's been a teacher, a conference leader, a public speaker, a children's minister, a deacon, an elder, a vacation Bible school coordinator, a preschool director, and a Bible study leader yet writing stories is just about the best way she can imagine spending her time.

Living in Bridgewater, New Jersey, with her husband of over twenty-five years and their three children, each of Sue's stories champions those emotions nearest and dearest to her: faith, joy, hope and love.

Philippians 1:20-21: *I earnestly expect and hope that I will in no way be ashamed but will have sufficient courage so that now, as always, Christ will be exalted in my life. For me, to live is Christ and to die is gain.*

Bibliography & Footnotes

Thanks to these wonderful Internet sites:

> www.biblegateway.com
>
> www.biblehub.com
>
> http://www.openbible.info/topics/

Thanks to these tremendous Bible translations that I regularly use and enjoy:

New Living Translation (NLT) *Holy Bible,* New Living Translation, copyright © 1996, 2004, 2015 by Tyndale House Foundation. Used by permission of Tyndale House Publishers Inc., Carol Stream, Illinois 60188. All rights reserved.

English Standard Version (ESV) The Holy Bible, English Standard Version. ESV® Permanent Text Edition® (2016). Copyright © 2001 by Crossway Bibles, a publishing ministry of Good News Publishers.

The Message (MSG) Copyright © 1993, 1994, 1995, 1996, 2000, 2001, 2002 by Eugene H. Peterson

New Century Version (NCV) The Holy Bible, New Century Version®. Copyright © 2005 by Thomas Nelson, Inc.

King James Version (KJV) (Public Domain)

New International Version (NIV) Holy Bible, New International Version®, NIV® Copyright ©1973, 1978, 1984, 2011 by Biblica, Inc.

Susan McGeown

---

[1] The Servant Song, by Richard Gillard of New Zealand, 1976-1977

[2] Sung by Mercy Me, "One Trick Pony" from the album Coming Up To Breathe, April 25, 2006, Fair Trade Services Label

[3] "Hymn" by Jars of Clay, from the album Much Afraid, September 16, 1997.

[4] *Great is Thy Faithfulness*, By Thomas O. Chisholm Great Is Thy Faithfulness is a popular Christian hymn written by Thomas Chisholm (1866–1960) with music composed by William M. Runyan (1870–1957) in Baldwin, Kansas, U.S.. The phrase "great is thy faithfulness" comes from the Old Testament Book of Lamentations 3:23. These exact words occur in both the King James Bible and the Revised Standard Version.

[5] Sung by Sara Groves, "Awakening" from the album Past the Wishing, copyright Sponge Records, September 20, 2011

[6] Sung by Laura Story, "Blessings" from the album Blessings. Written by Liz Story • Copyright © Warner/Chappell Music, Inc, Universal Music Publishing Group, March 4, 2016

[7] *It Is Well With My Soul,* Horatio G. Spafford, 1873 "Horatio G. Spafford was a successful lawyer and businessman in Chicago with a lovely family — a wife, Anna, and five children. However, they were not strangers to tears and tragedy. Their young son died with pneumonia in 1871, and in that same year, much of their business was lost in the great Chicago fire. Yet, God in His mercy and kindness allowed the business to flourish once more.

On Nov. 21, 1873, the French ocean liner, Ville du Havre was crossing the Atlantic from the U.S. to Europe with 313 passengers on board. Among the passengers were Mrs. Spafford and their four daughters. Although Mr. Spafford had planned to go with his family, he found it necessary to stay in Chicago to help solve an unexpected business problem. He told his wife he would join her and their children in Europe a few days later. His plan was to take another ship.

About four days into the crossing of the Atlantic, the Ville du Harve collided with a powerful, iron-hulled Scottish ship, the Loch Earn. Suddenly, all of those on board were in grave danger. Anna hurriedly brought her four children to the deck. She knelt there with Annie, Margaret Lee, Bessie and Tanetta and prayed that God would spare them if that could be His will, or to make them willing to endure whatever awaited them. Within approximately 12 minutes, the Ville du Harve slipped beneath the dark waters of the Atlantic, carrying with it 226 of the passengers including the four Spafford children.

A sailor, rowing a small boat over the spot where the ship went down, spotted a woman floating on a piece of the wreckage. It was Anna, still alive. He pulled her into the boat and they were picked up by another large vessel which, nine days later, landed them in Cardiff, Wales. From there she wired her husband a message which began, "Saved alone, what shall I do?" Mr. Spafford later framed the telegram and placed it in his office.

Another of the ship's survivors, Pastor Weiss, later recalled Anna saying, "God gave me four daughters. Now they have been taken from me. Someday I will understand why."

Mr. Spafford booked passage on the next available ship and left to join his grieving wife. With the ship about four days out, the captain called Spafford to his cabin and told him they were over the place where his children went down.

According to Bertha Spafford Vester, a daughter born after the tragedy, Spafford wrote "It Is Well With My Soul" while on this journey.

[8] *Doubly Good To You* sung by Amy Grant, found on her Straight Ahead album, August 14, 2007, Amy Grant records

[9] *Amazing Grace* written by John Newton, published in 1779, Newton wrote the words from personal experience. He grew up without any particular religious conviction, but his life's path was formed by a variety of twists and coincidences that were often put into motion by his recalcitrant insubordination. He was pressed (conscripted) into service in the Royal Navy, and after leaving the service, he became involved in the Atlantic slave trade. In 1748, a violent storm battered his vessel off the coast of County Donegal, Ireland, so severely that he called out to God for mercy, a moment that marked his spiritual conversion. He continued his slave trading career until 1754 or 1755, when he ended his seafaring altogether and began studying Christian theology.

[10] *Sacred Delight*, By the band Sunday Drive on the album Sunday Drive, August 3, 2009, Brentwood Music

[11] *Clay and Water*, from the album Falling Forward by Margaret Becker, Sparrow label, April 21, 1998

---

[12] *Blest Be The Tie That Binds*, written by Rev. John Fawcett (1739-1817). Rev. John Fawcett (1739-1817) was a young preacher in Wainsgate, which seemed then to be the middle of nowhere. (Think *Wuthering Heights*.) The Yorkshire countryside in Northern England was barren and cold.

The people — goodhearted, hardworking, mostly illiterate — had next to nothing. They supplemented their pastor's meager stipend with wool and potatoes. Nor was there a parsonage. Instead, Fawcett, his wife and four children were passed from one family to the next, a few months here, a few months there, no place to call their own. They suffered chilly drafts and ate porridge with their host families.

Poverty was nothing new to Fawcett. Orphaned at 12, he became an indentured servant at 13, worked 14 hours a day, and taught himself to read at night. When he was 15, he stood in an outdoor crowd of 20,000 to hear a sermon by George Whitefield, "the marvel of the age," and set his mind on becoming a preacher.

One day in 1772, after seven years of pastoring in Yorkshire, 33-year-old Fawcett got the call. He had established a reputation as a theologian, inspiring preacher, and serious scholar and was now wanted in London. London!

It seemed a dream come true, to move to lively London where his family's standard of living would vastly improve. The city had good schools, libraries, sophisticated music and art, churches with stained glass, and educated colleagues for deep conversation. Fawcett agonized over the tempting offer and finally said YES!

The family packed up, climbed into a wagon, and waved to people who had come many miles to say goodbye. The scene was so wrenching, however, that Fawcett realized he couldn't leave. He turned the horses around, unpacked, and stayed in Yorkshire for another 45 years.

Out of this experience, he wrote the most famous of his 160 hymns, "Blest Be the Tie that Binds." It became a favorite hymn for Christians facing separation, an affirmation that friendship and community are the true measures of wealth.

[13] "Faithful To Me" by Jennifer Knapp from her album "Kansas" November 4, 2008

[14] "Valleys Fill First" by Caedmon's Call from the album "Long Line of Leavers", May 15, 2001

---

[15] "Brave" by Nichole Nordeman, from her album "Brave", 2005

[16] "Faith Enough" by Jars of Clay, from the album Who We Are Instead, November 4, 2003 Inspired by the Ernest Hemingway quote, "The world breaks everyone and afterward many are strong at the broken places," from A Farewell To Arms

[17] New Living Translation (NLT) Holy Bible, New Living Translation, copyright © 1996, 2004, 2015 by Tyndale House Foundation. Used by permission of Tyndale House Publishers Inc., Carol Stream, Illinois 60188. All rights reserved. PLEASE NOTE ALL SCRIPTURE IS FROM THE NEW LIVING TRANSLATION UNLESS OTHERWISE NOTED.

[18] All quotations from Oswald Chambers are from his devotional book *My Utmost For His Highest*, first published in 1935. It comes in various formats and revisions and has been translated into over 39 languages.

[19] C.S. Lewis was a prolific author and speaker who lived from 1898 to 1963. Unless noted, the majority of quotes in this booklet will be from his book *Mere Christianity* which was a culmination of radio talks he made between 1941 to 1944. Quotes related to other writings will be identified as such.

[20] C.S. Lewis, The Four Loves

[21] Mother Teresa, known in the Catholic Church as Saint Teresa of Calcutta[6] (born Anjezë Gonxhe Bojaxhiu; Albanian; 26 August 1910 – 5 September 1997), was an Albanian-Indian[4] Roman Catholic nun and missionary. She was born in Skopje (now the capital of the Republic of Macedonia), then part of the Kosovo Vilayet of the Ottoman Empire. After living in Macedonia for eighteen years she moved to Ireland and then to India, where she lived for most of her life.

In 1950 Teresa founded the Missionaries of Charity, a Roman Catholic religious congregation which had over 4,500 sisters and was active in 133 countries in 2012. The congregation manages homes for people dying of HIV/AIDS, leprosy and tuberculosis; soup kitchens; dispensaries and mobile clinics; children's- and family-counselling programmes; orphanages, and schools. Members, who take vows of chastity, poverty, and obedience, also profess a fourth vow: to give "wholehearted free service to the poorest of the poor".

---

[22] All quotes from Rick Warren are from his devotional book *The Purpose Driven Life (What On Earth Am I Here For?)* published by Zondervan publishers. ISBN: 978-0310205715

[23] Elisabeth Elliot (née Howard; December 21, 1926 – June 15, 2015) was a Christian author and speaker. Her first husband, Jim Elliot, was killed in 1956 while attempting to make missionary contact with the Auca (now known as Huaorani; also rendered as Waorani or Waodani) of eastern Ecuador. She later spent two years as a missionary to the tribe members who killed her husband. Returning to the United States after many years in South America, she became widely known as the author of over twenty books and as a speaker. Elliot toured the country, sharing her knowledge and experience, well into her seventies.

[24] Cornelia "Corrie" ten Boom (15 April 1892 – 15 April 1983) was a Dutch watchmaker and Christian who, along with her father and other family members, helped many Jews escape the Nazi Holocaust during World War II. She was imprisoned for her actions. Her most famous book, The Hiding Place, is a biography that recounts the story of her family's efforts, as well as her time spent in a concentration camp.

[25] A. W. Tozer was another prolific writer who lived from 1897 to 1963. His books *How To Be Filled With The Holy Spirit* and *The Pursuit of God* are invaluable resources in my life.

[26] *Mornings With The Holy Spirit*, by Jennifer LeClaire, Charisma House Publishers, 2015, ISBN 978-1-62998-189-5

[27] Philip Yancey is another prolific contemporary author. All the quotes in this section, however, are from his excellent book, *Prayer Does It Make Any Difference*, published by Zondervan, 2006, ISBN 978-0-310-27105-5

[28] From Timothy Keller's excellent book, *The Reason For God, Belief in an Age of Skepticism*, by Riverhead Books, New York, 2008, ISBN 978-0-525-95049-3

[29] St. Patrick's Breastplate is a popular prayer attributed to one of Ireland's most beloved patron saints. According to tradition, St. Patrick wrote it in 433 A.D. for divine protection before successfully converting the Irish King Leoghaire and his subjects from paganism to Christianity. (The term breastplate refers to a piece of armor worn in battle.)

More recent scholarship suggests its author was anonymous. In any case, this prayer certainly reflects the spirit with which St. Patrick brought our faith to Ireland! St. Patrick's Breastplate, also known as *The Lorica of Saint Patrick* was popular enough to inspire a hymn based on this text as well. (This prayer has also been called *The Cry of the Deer.*)

[30] In 1927 American writer Max Ehrmann (1872–1945) wrote the prose poem *Desiderata*, which was first published in *The Poems of Max Ehrmann* in 1948. In 1956, the Reverend Frederick Kates, rector of Saint Paul's Church in Baltimore, Maryland, included *Desiderata* in a compilation of devotional materials for his congregation. The compilation included the church's foundation date: "Old Saint Paul's Church, Baltimore AD 1692". Consequently, the date of the text's authorship was (and still is) widely mistaken as 1692, the year of the church's foundation.

[31] Empower Me, by Ted Loder, from *Wrestling the Light,* http://myblog-everydaygraces.blogspot.com/2011/12/empower-me-to-be-bold-participant.html

[32] From the book by John Ortberg called, "If you Want To Walk on Water, You've Got to Get Out of the Boat", Zondervan Publishers, May, 2014, ISBN 978-031-283379

[33] From the poem, "What I live For" by George Linnaeus Banks

[34] Edward McKendree Bounds (August 15, 1835 – August 24, 1913) prominently known as E.M. Bounds, was an American author, attorney, and member of the Methodist Episcopal Church South clergy. He is known for writing 11 books, nine of which focused on the subject of prayer. Only two of Bounds' books were published before he died. After his death, Rev. Claudius (Claude) Lysias Chilton, Jr., grandson of William Parish Chilton and admirer of Bounds, worked on preserving and preparing Bounds' collection of manuscripts for publication. By 1921, more editorial work was being done by Rev. Homer W. Hodge.

Susan McGeown

BIBLE EMERGENCY NUMBERS

"My presence shall go with thee, and I will give thee rest" (Exodus 33:14)

When in sorrow, call John 14
When men fail you, call Psalm 27
When you have sinned, call Psalm 51
When you worry, call Matthew 6:19-34
When you are in danger, call Psalm 91
When God seems far away, call Psalm 139
When your faith needs stirring, call Hebrew 11
When you are lonely and fearful, call Psalm 23
When you grow bitter and critical, call 1 Cor. 13
When you feel down and out, call Romans 8:31-39
When you want peace and rest, call Matthew 11:25-30
When the world seems bigger than God, call Psalm 90
When you want Christian assurance, call Romans 8:1-30
When you leave home for labor or travel, call Psalm 121
When your prayers grow narrow or selfish, call Psalm 67
When you want courage for a task, call Joshua 1
When you think of investments/returns, call Mark 10
How to get along with fellowmen, call Romans 12
For great invention/opportunity, call Isaiah 55
For Paul's secret to happiness, call Col. 3:12-17
For idea of Christianity, call 1 Cor 5:15-19
If you are depressed, call Psalm 27
If you want to be fruitful, call John 15
If your pocketbook is empty, call Psalm 37
If your losing confidence in people, call 1Cor. 13
If people seem unkind, call John 15
If discouraged about your work, call Psalm 126
If you find the world growing small, and you great, call Psalm 19